HOW TO DRAW™
PERSPECTIVE

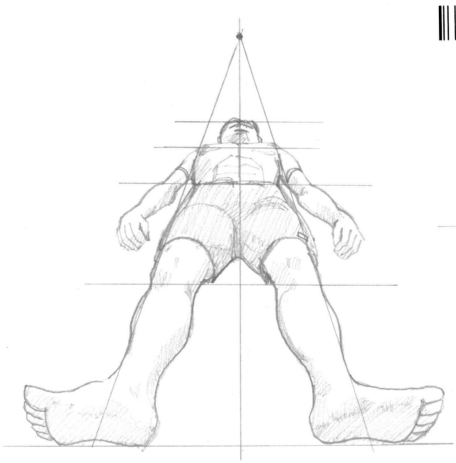

Mark Bergin

BOOK HOUSE

Published in Great Britain in MMXIII by
Book House, an imprint of
The Salariya Book Company Ltd
25 Marlborough Place, Brighton BN1 1UB
www.salariya.com

ISBN: 978-1-908973-45-0

7 9 8 6

A CIP catalogue record for this book is available
from the British Library.

Printed and bound in China.

Reprinted in MMXVIII.

Author: **Mark Bergin** was born in Hastings
in 1961. He studied at Eastbourne College of Art
and has specialised in historical reconstructions as
well as aviation and maritime subjects since 1983.
He lives in Bexhill-on-Sea with his wife and
three children.

Editor: Rob Walker

Visit
www.salariya.com
for our online catalogue and
free fun stuff.

PAPER FROM
SUSTAINABLE
FORESTS

**WARNING: Fixatives should be used
only under adult supervision.**

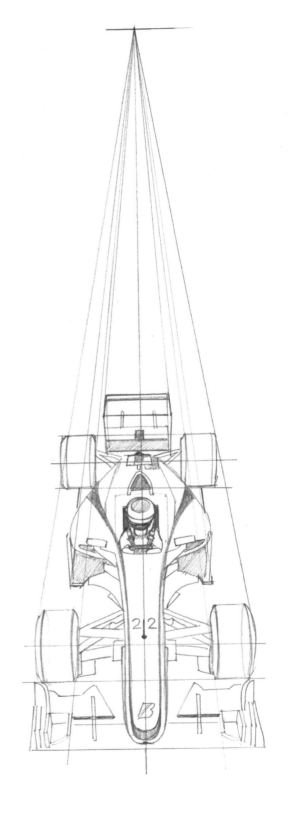

Contents

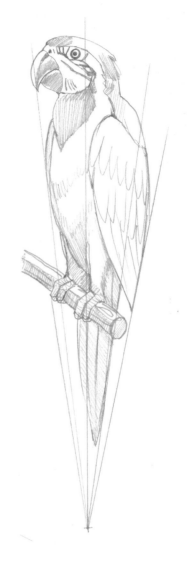

What is perspective?

Perspective is a way of drawing things so that they appear to be in three dimensions. When you look at an object in real life, the parts of it that are close to your eye look larger than the parts that are further away. Things that are really the same width, such as railway lines, appear to get narrower as they vanish into the distance. If you copy this effect in your drawing, you can trick the eye into seeing in 3D.

These trees are all the same height, but the further ones look smaller and closer together than the nearer ones. The two rows of trees are parallel, but perspective makes them appear to meet in the far distance. This is an example of simple one–point perspective (see pages 6—7).

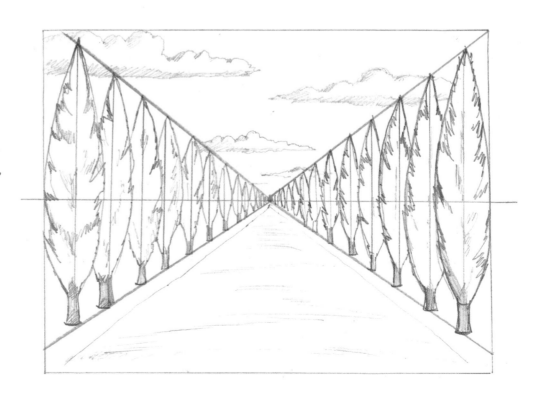

Imagine you are looking through a window at an object in the distance. Rays of light from the object pass through the window and reach your eyes. If you could trace exactly what you see on the glass, you would have a picture in perfect perspective.

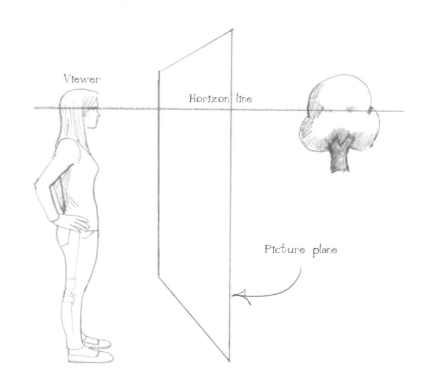

The **horizon** is the line in the far distance where earth and sky seem to meet. It is always level with the viewer's eye. The **picture plane** is that imaginary window between the viewer and the object viewed.

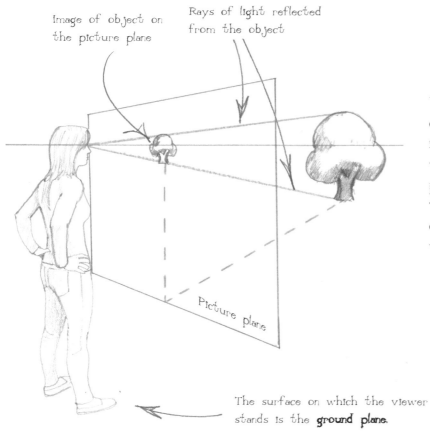

You see the object through the rays of light that are reflected off it. The image you want to draw is formed where these rays of light meet the picture plane. The distance between the viewer, the picture plane and the object determines how big the object will appear in the final drawing.

Vanishing points

The place in the far distance where parallel lines appear to meet is the **vanishing point**. In simple one-point perspective there is only one vanishing point, and it is on the horizon.

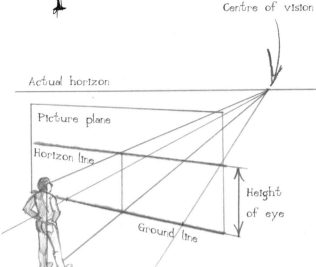

The **horizon line** in the picture is where the light rays reflected from the actual horizon meet the picture plane. The horizon is always level with the viewer's **eye level** (the height of the viewer's eye above the ground plane). The **centre of vision** is the point on the horizon exactly opposite the viewer's eye. The **ground line** is where the picture plane meets the ground plane.

One-point perspective

In one-point perspective, lines that lead away from the viewer (such as the sides of the road in this picture) meet at the vanishing point on the horizon. Vertical or horizontal lines that are parallel to the viewer (such as the walls of the buildings facing us) remain vertical or horizontal in the picture as well.

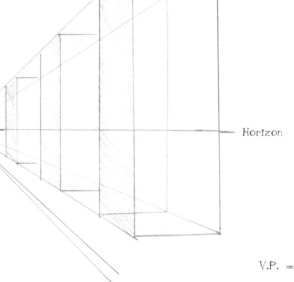

V.P. = vanishing point

One-point perspective is used when one side of the object is parallel to the viewer, such as when you are looking at a building head-on. If the object is at an angle to the viewer, such as when you are standing to one side of a building and looking at the corner of it, you need to use two-point perspective.

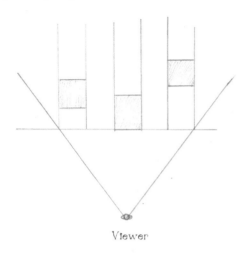

Viewer

In this plan view we see a person looking at three buildings. One side of each building faces the viewer.

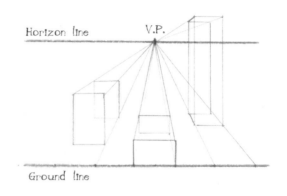

This is how the viewer sees the three buildings, in one-point perspective.

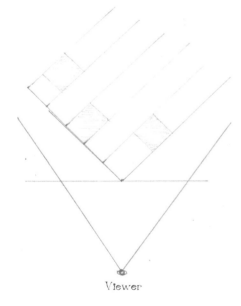

Viewer

In this plan view, the person is looking from the corner and can see two sides of each building.

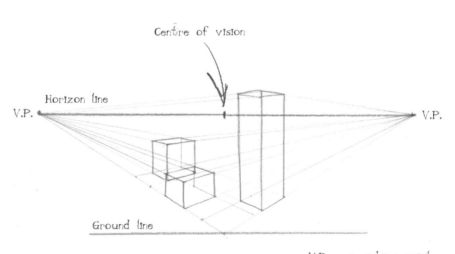

This is how the three buildings appear to the viewer in two-point perspective.

Changing viewpoints

These examples all show the same cube drawn from different positions.

In the examples on this page, the front face of the cube is parallel to the viewer. The viewer sees the cube in one-point perspective.

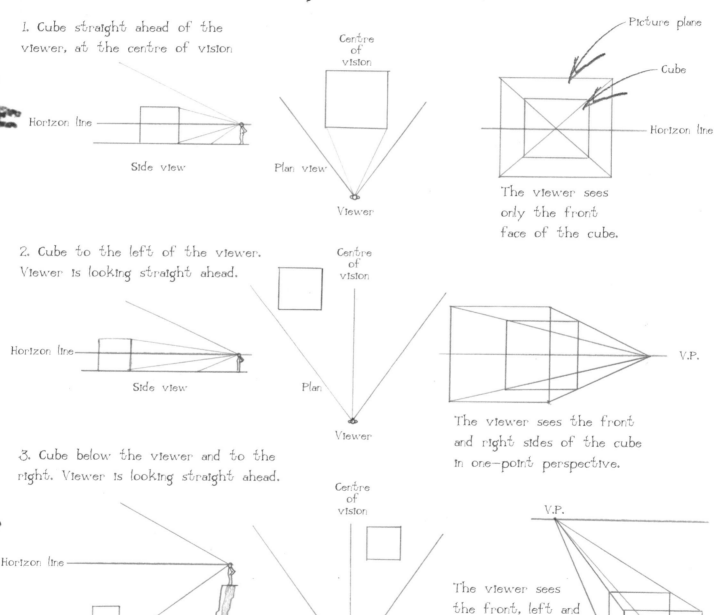

1. Cube straight ahead of the viewer, at the centre of vision

Centre of vision

Horizon line

Side view

Plan view

Viewer

Picture plane

Cube

Horizon line

The viewer sees only the front face of the cube.

2. Cube to the left of the viewer. Viewer is looking straight ahead.

Centre of vision

Horizon line

Side view

Plan

Viewer

V.P.

The viewer sees the front and right sides of the cube in one-point perspective.

3. Cube below the viewer and to the right. Viewer is looking straight ahead.

Centre of vision

Horizon line

Viewer standing on a high place

Side view

Plan

Viewer

V.P.

The viewer sees the front, left and top faces of the cube in one-point perspective.

Two-point perspective

In the examples on this page, the cube is turned so that the viewer can see two sides at once. Each side converges towards its own separate vanishing point on the horizon. This is called two-point perspective. In two-point perspective, lines which are vertical on the real object are vertical in the drawing also.

1. The cube is directly opposite the viewer, with two sides facing the viewer.

Side view

Plan

Viewer

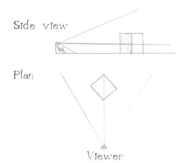

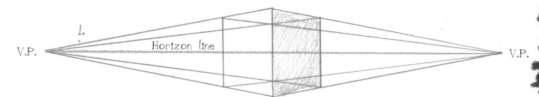

The viewer sees two sides of the cube in two-point perspective. Because the cube is at the centre of vision, the viewer sees equal amounts of both sides.

2. The cube is directly opposite the viewer, and below the viewer's eye level.

Side view

Plan

Viewer standing on a high place

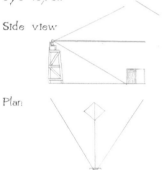

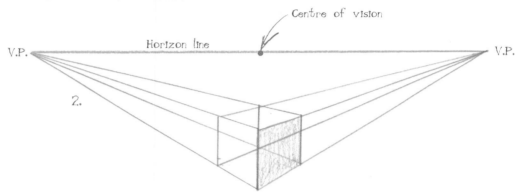

The viewer sees two sides and the top of the cube in two-point perspective. Again the viewer sees equal amounts of both sides of the cube.

3. The cube is to the right of the viewer, and above the viewer's eye level.

Side view

Plan

Viewer

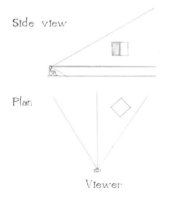

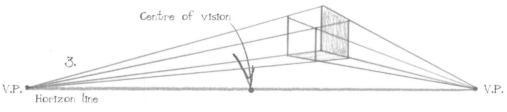

The viewer sees two sides and the underside of the cube in two-point perspective. Because the cube is to the right of the centre of vision, the viewer sees more of the left side of the cube than the right side.

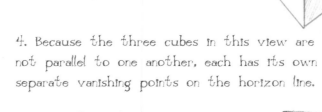

4. Because the three cubes in this view are not parallel to one another, each has its own separate vanishing points on the horizon line.

9

Looking up or down

Three—point perspective is used when the viewpoint is either very low or very high. Aerial or ground—level photos of skyscrapers create dramatic viewpoints that are a good way of showing how three—point perspective works.

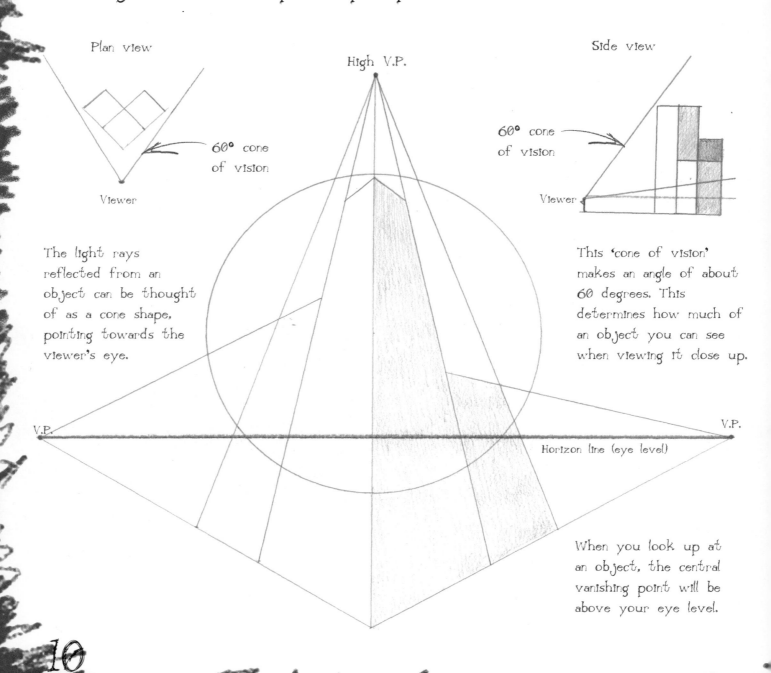

Plan view

60° cone of vision

Viewer

The light rays reflected from an object can be thought of as a cone shape, pointing towards the viewer's eye.

High V.P.

Side view

60° cone of vision

Viewer

This 'cone of vision' makes an angle of about 60 degrees. This determines how much of an object you can see when viewing it close up.

V.P.

V.P.

Horizon line (eye level)

When you look up at an object, the central vanishing point will be above your eye level.

A high—level view means that the sides of the buildings dramatically converge towards a low vanishing point. The tops of the buildings will also be visible.

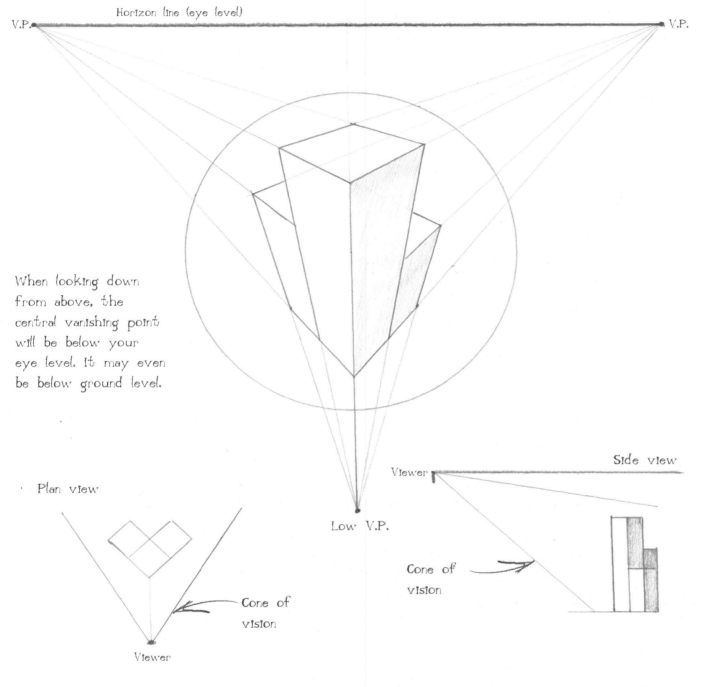

V.P.   Horizon line (eye level)   V.P.

When looking down from above, the central vanishing point will be below your eye level. It may even be below ground level.

Low V.P.

Plan view

Cone of vision

Viewer

Side view

Viewer

Cone of vision

In three—point perspective, lines which are vertical or horizontal in real life (such as the walls of these skyscrapers) are always shown sloping in the drawing, unless they are exactly in line with the centre of vision.

11

Circles and ellipses

When a circle is seen in perspective it usually appears as an ellipse (oval). Circles become progressively more elliptical when viewed at more acute angles.

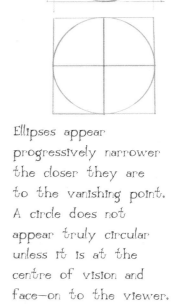

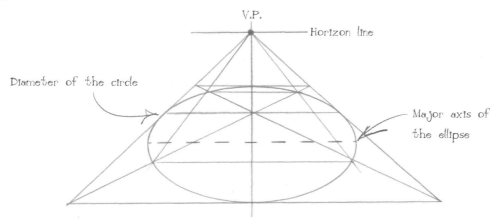

Horizon line

V.P.

Diameter of the circle

Major axis of the ellipse

When a circle is drawn in perspective, the diameter (the widest part of the circle) is always further away than you think. It is always closer to the V.P. than the major axis (centre line) of the ellipse.

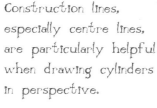

Construction lines, especially centre lines, are particularly helpful when drawing cylinders in perspective.

Ellipses appear progressively narrower the closer they are to the vanishing point. A circle does not appear truly circular unless it is at the centre of vision and face—on to the viewer.

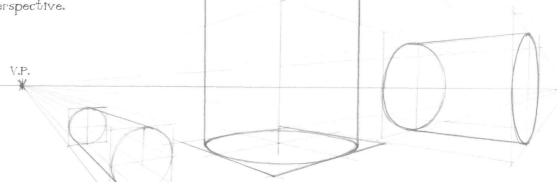

V.P.

V.P.

12

Always use centre lines and
other construction lines to
help you get ellipses right.

Many everyday objects are
based on cylinders and circles.
Viewed in perspective, all
these shapes become ellipses.

Practice in drawing
ellipses will help to make
your drawings more
convincing and three—
dimensional.

Draw the whole of the ellipse —
even the parts that are hidden
behind other objects — to give
your drawing a solid structure.

13

Distance and height

ere's how to draw a group of people all standing at different distances from the viewer.

The first thing to notice is that all the surfers are about the same height as the viewer. This means that they all have the same eye level, and it is on the horizon line.

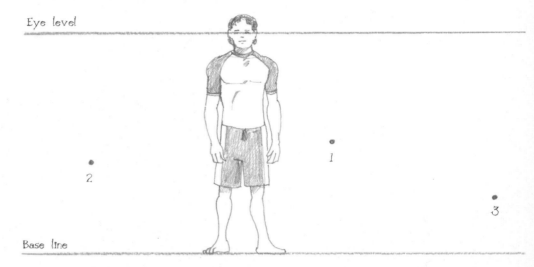

The figure nearest the viewer is drawn first. Points 1, 2 and 3 show where the other surfers are to stand.

Draw a vertical line (AB) through the centre of the figure. Draw a line from B through point 1 and extend it till it meets the eye—level line. This is the vanishing point for the first two surfers. Now draw a line from A to the same vanishing point.

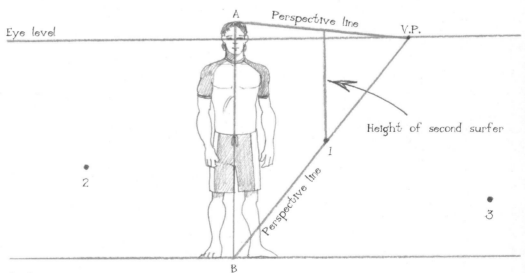

The two lines you have just drawn are perspective lines. Between the two perspective lines, draw a vertical line with its base on point 1. This gives you the height of the second surfer.

Draw the second surfer, keeping the same proportions as the first figure.

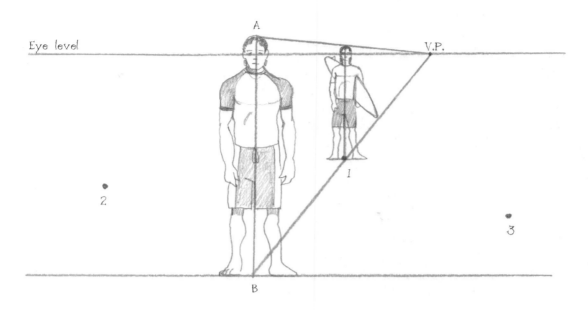

To find the height of the figure standing at point 2:

(1) Draw a horizontal line from 2 that meets the lower perspective line.

(2) Draw a vertical line up from there to meet the higher perspective line.

(3) Draw a second horizontal line from here to show where the top of the third figure's head should be.

Repeat these three steps at point 3 to work out the height of the fourth figure.

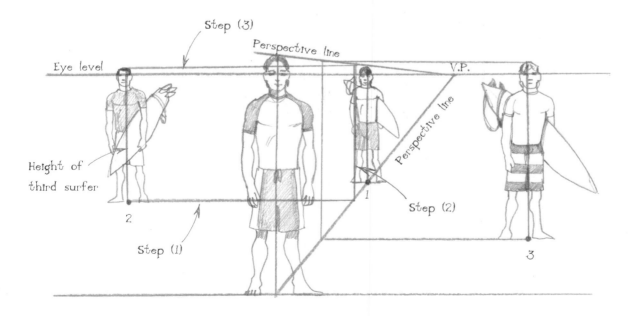

Figures in perspective

Perspective does not only apply to cubes and simple geometric shapes. The easiest way to draw complex shapes in perspective is to imagine that they are surrounded by a grid of parallel lines, or contained in a rectangular box.

One—point perspective

Construct a grid to help you with the foreshortening of the limbs, body and head.

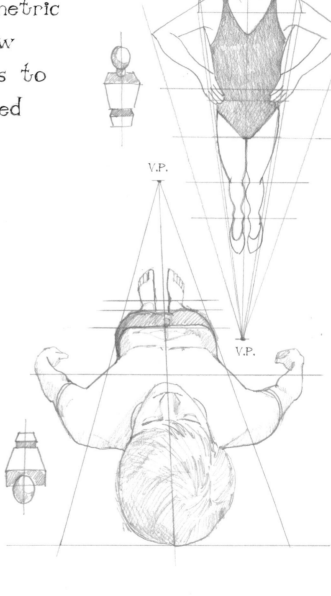

V.P.

V.P.

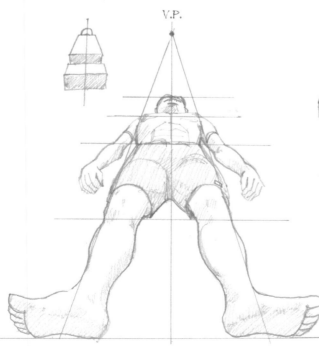

V.P.

The spacing between gridlines progressively widens as they come closer to the viewer.

Two-point perspective

There is one vanishing point for lines running across the width of the body and another for lines running along its length.

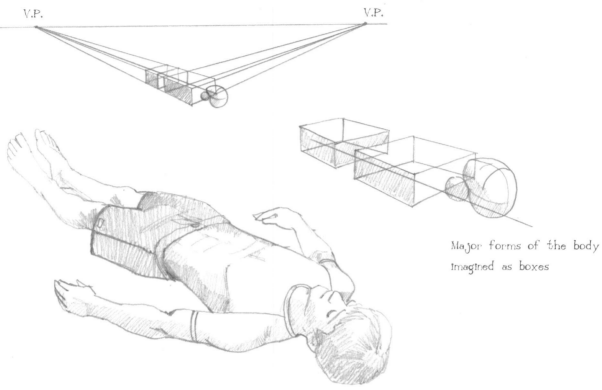

Major forms of the body imagined as boxes

Three-point perspective

A figure viewed from above or below requires three vanishing points.

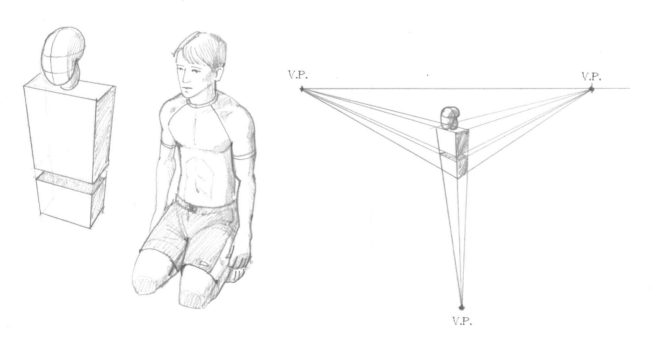

Animals in perspective

Drawing animals in perspective can be difficult because of their irregular forms. The use of grids and box construction can help you to find vanishing points and horizon lines.

This parrot is viewed close up from above. You can make the most of drawing from observation by using an implied vanishing point below.

Sketch the animal's body as a rectangular box drawn in perspective.

Constructing a box around the major body shapes of an animal can help you find a vanishing point.

V.P.

V.P.

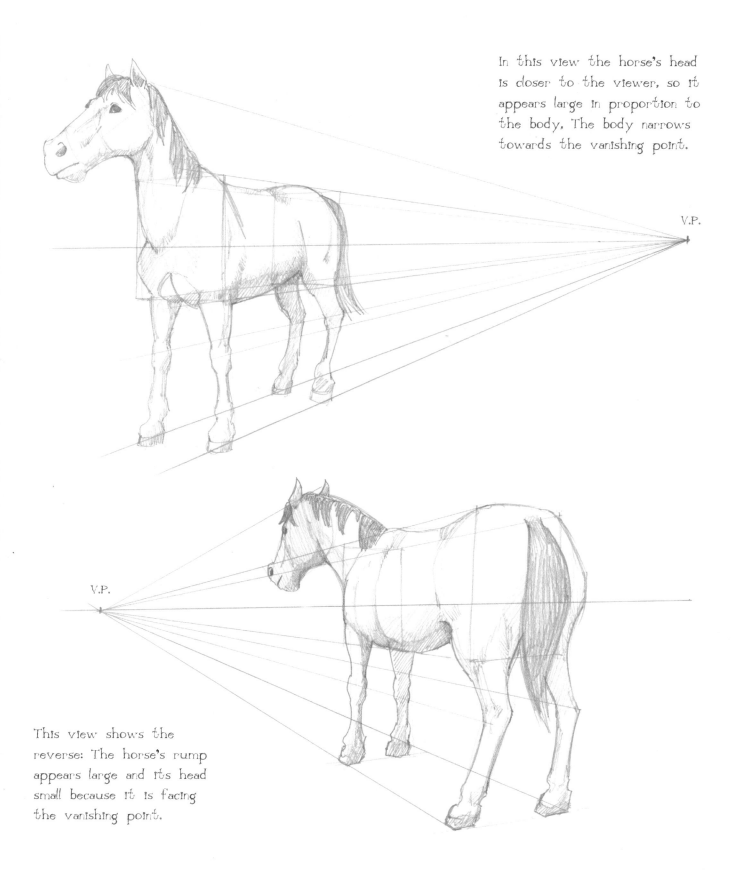

In this view the horse's head is closer to the viewer, so it appears large in proportion to the body, The body narrows towards the vanishing point.

V.P.

V.P.

This view shows the reverse: The horse's rump appears large and its head small because it is facing the vanishing point.

19

Boats and ships

Some boats and ships look difficult to draw. A good tip for drawing any vessel is to simplify its shape into a box or an oblong. Then sketch in the details of the stern, bow and other parts.

In the drawing of the rowing boat, the red line shows how it would look if the top were sliced off flat. Note how the bow and stern shapes rise above the red line. This gives the sweeping curves typical of a rowing boat.

Stern

Bow

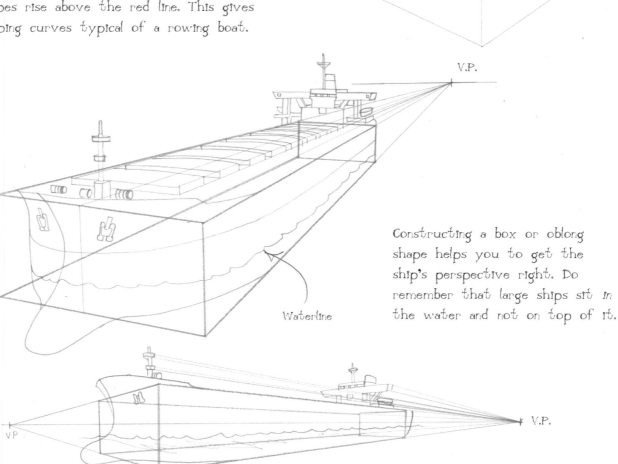

V.P.

Constructing a box or oblong shape helps you to get the ship's perspective right. Do remember that large ships sit in the water and not on top of it.

Waterline

V.P.

VP

This page shows the same racing yacht in two different views. One is in two-point, the other in three-point perspective. Note that the spinnaker curves are very different in each view. Also observe how much deck is shown in the high eye-level view (below).

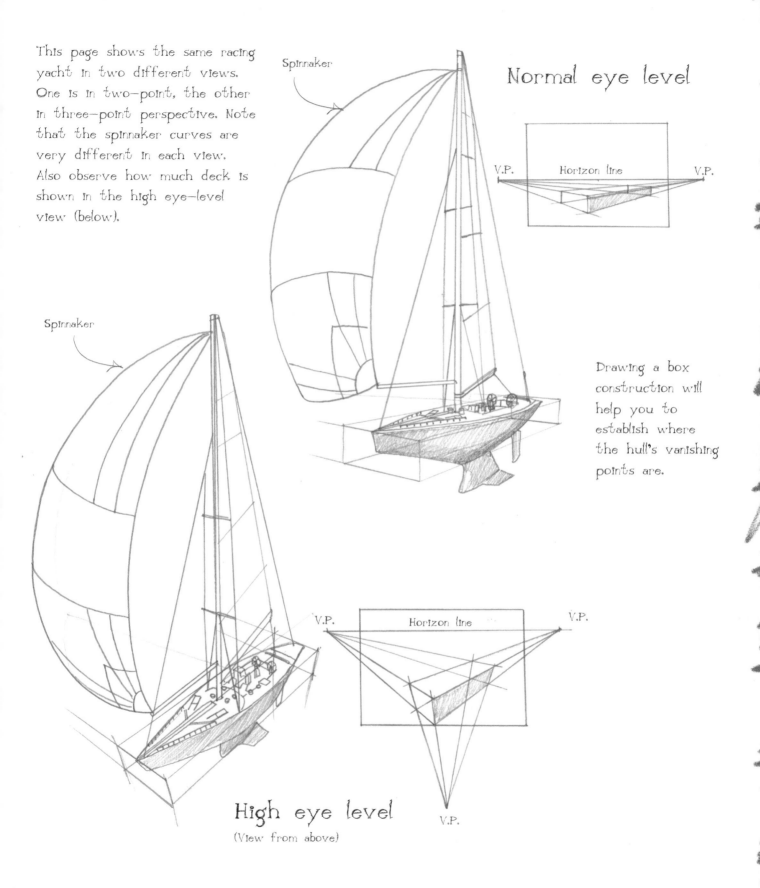

Spinnaker

Normal eye level

V.P.   Horizon line   V.P.

Spinnaker

Drawing a box construction will help you to establish where the hull's vanishing points are.

V.P.   Horizon line   V.P.

V.P.

High eye level
(View from above)

Cars in perspective

Cars with a cuboid shape are fairly easy to draw in perspective. Open-wheeled cars are more difficult to get right, but drawing a box shape will help.

V.P.
Horizon line

This view is good for a race scene, as the car looks as though it is heading straight for the viewer. This creates the feeling of being in the midst of the action.

V.P.
Horizon line

When tyres are viewed head—on they look like rectangles. When viewed from an angle, they become ellipses (see pages 12—13). The nose and front wheels of this car appear large because they are close to the viewer.

A higher eye level creates less impact in this case, as the car appears more distant.

V.P. Horizon line V.P.

This Le Mans sports car is easy to draw beause of its strong cuboid shape. This makes it easier to see the vanishing points.

A three-quarter view makes this car look interesting and stylish. It is worth taking time to work out the correct positions of the wheels using construction lines, as this will give your drawing a more solid feel.

Axle

Axle

Sketching the positions of the axles will help to make sure that the wheels and other parts are correctly aligned.

Tyre seen head-on   Tyre seen at an angle

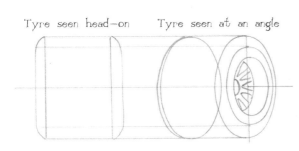

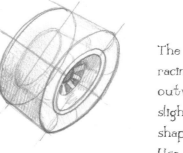

The tyre walls of many racing cars bow outwards, which slightly alters the shapes of the ellipses. Use construction lines to define the form of the tyres.

Find the centre of the wheel by drawing the axle first; it will make drawing ellipses easier.

23

Uphill, downhill

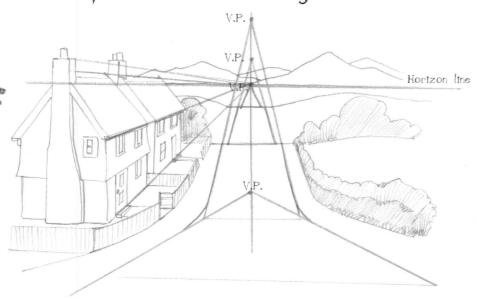

Valleys and hills add movement and rhythm to a landscape. Drawing the road and buildings in perspective leads the viewer's eye from the foreground into the far distance.

As the road climbs to the horizon, each separate incline has its own vanishing point which converges along the central line of vision.

This downhill view of a street by the seafront has a clear horizon line. This can be used to position the centre of vision and all the different vanishing points.

Street scene: Mermaid Street, Rye, East Sussex

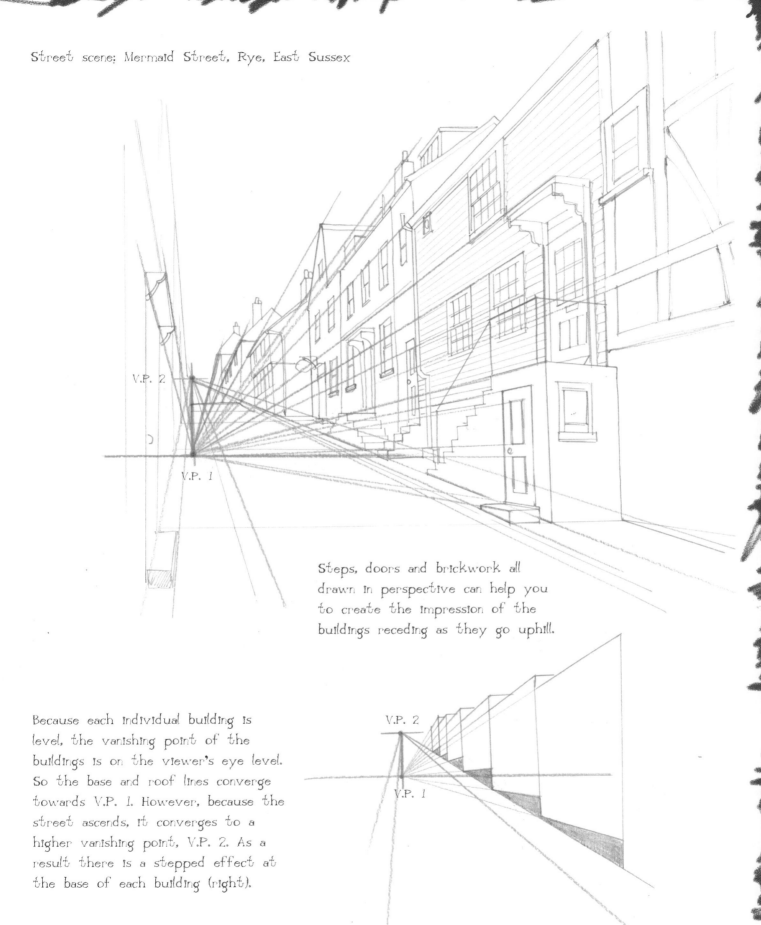

V.P. 2

V.P. 1

Steps, doors and brickwork all
drawn in perspective can help you
to create the impression of the
buildings receding as they go uphill.

Because each individual building is
level, the vanishing point of the
buildings is on the viewer's eye level.
So the base and roof lines converge
towards V.P. 1. However, because the
street ascends, it converges to a
higher vanishing point, V.P. 2. As a
result there is a stepped effect at
the base of each building (right).

V.P. 2

V.P. 1

25

Reflections

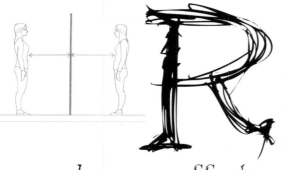

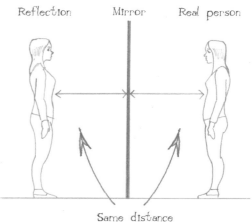
Reflection   Mirror   Real person

Same distance

Reflected images are difficult but can be very effective if observed well. A reflection in a window or a mirror will appear to be the same distance behind the glass as the real object is in front of it.

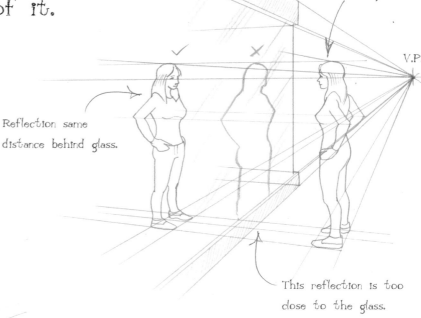

Real person

V.P.

Reflection same distance behind glass.

This reflection is too close to the glass.

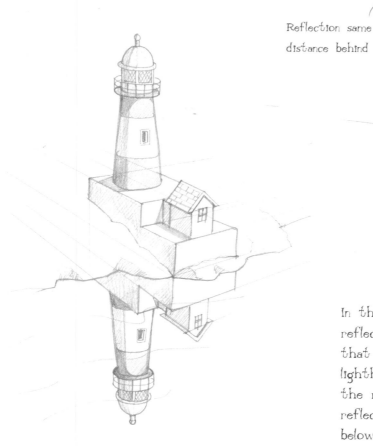

In the lighthouse drawing, both the building and its reflection have the same vanishing points. Note that the reflection shows the underside of the lighthouse platform, not the top. This is because the rays of light that reach the viewer's eye are reflected from the surface of the water, which is below the lighthouse.

In these sketches, compare the subject of the drawing with its reflection by turning the book upside down. See how the roof of the boat and the reflected roof share the same vanishing point.

Similarly, the roofs of the houses converge towards the same vanishing point as the roofs in the reflected image.

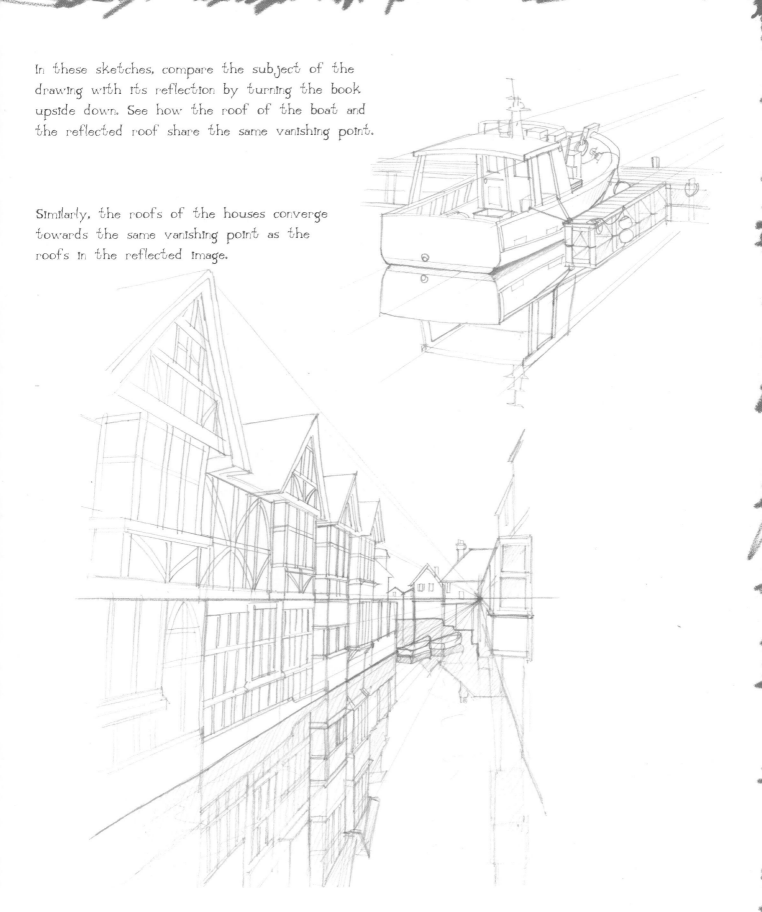

Light and shadow

ight is crucial to the way we view objects, as their 3D form is created by light and shade. Without a light source, you see only darkness. Even in low lighting conditions it is hard to judge the size and position of an object.

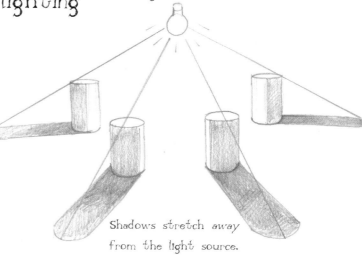

Shadows form on the side of the object that faces away from the light source. In this example, light from front right casts a shadow to the left and behind.

Light source

Shadows stretch away from the light source.

The length of the shadow cast by an object is determined by the height and direction of the light source.

Light source

V.P.   V.P.   V.P.   V.P.

V.P.

The front edge of this shadow recedes towards the vanishing point above right.

The vanishing point for these shadows is positioned vertically below the lightbulb.

Draw lines from the lightbulb to the front corners of the box and extend these to the ground plane.

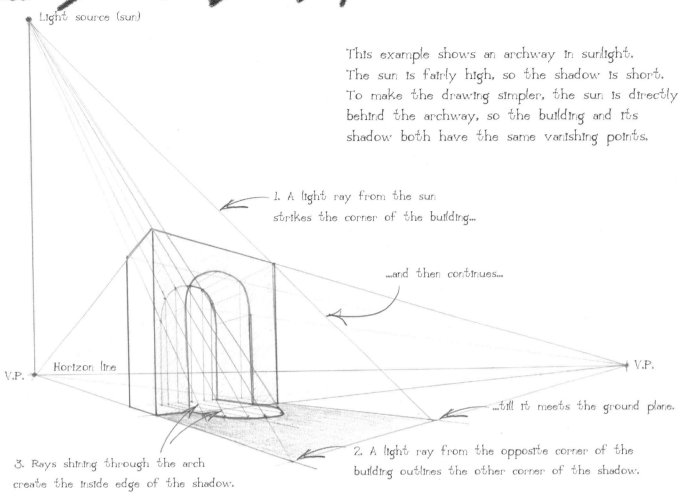

Light source (sun)

This example shows an archway in sunlight. The sun is fairly high, so the shadow is short. To make the drawing simpler, the sun is directly behind the archway, so the building and its shadow both have the same vanishing points.

1. A light ray from the sun strikes the corner of the building...

...and then continues...

V.P.   Horizon line   V.P.

...till it meets the ground plane.

3. Rays shining through the arch create the inside edge of the shadow.

2. A light ray from the opposite corner of the building outlines the other corner of the shadow.

In this more complicated example the sun is coming from the right and from behind the viewer. Because the light is coming from one side, the vanishing point for the building (V.P.) is not the same as the vanishing point for the shadow (V.P.S.). The sun's rays have their own vanishing point (V.P.S.R.) directly below the V.P.S.

To find the shape of the inside edge of the shadow:

1. Divide up the archway using a series of vertical lines which go down to the ground plane.

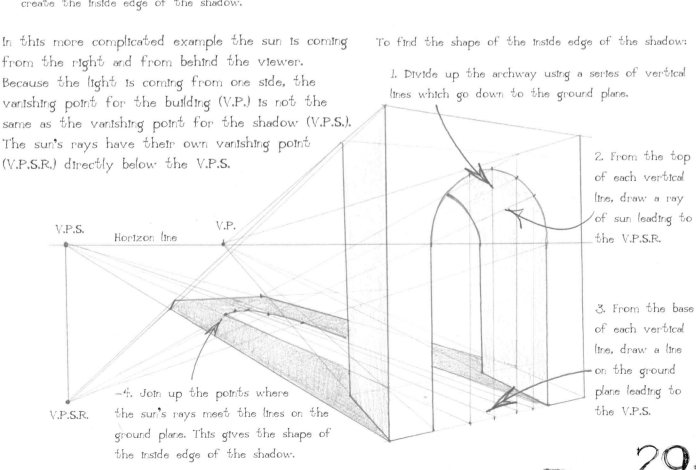

V.P.S.   Horizon line   V.P.

V.P.S.R.

2. From the top of each vertical line, draw a ray of sun leading to the V.P.S.R.

3. From the base of each vertical line, draw a line on the ground plane leading to the V.P.S.

4. Join up the points where the sun's rays meet the lines on the ground plane. This gives the shape of the inside edge of the shadow.

29

Landscapes

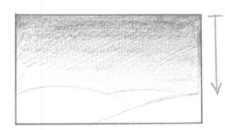

Careful use of tone in a landscape drawing can create a powerful feeling of scale and perspective.

Light rays at sunset or sunrise may give a perspective-like effect.

In this drawing (below right) the horizon line is very low, emphasising the mass of clouds. Note how the nearer clouds appear much larger than the further ones. In real life, clouds often form straight rows (weather experts call them 'cloud streets') which appear to converge to a vanishing point on the horizon.

Create a sense of depth in the landscape by gradually lightening the tone of the sky as it approaches the horizon line. Aim for a smooth transition from dark to light, as in the small diagram above.

In real life, very distant objects look paler (and often bluer) than nearby objects, because of the way light is scattered by the atmosphere. When this effect is used in art, it is called **atmospheric** or **aerial perspective**. Leonardo da Vinci is famous for using aerial perspective to give an illusion of depth in his paintings.

A good way to visualise a landscape composition is to think of it as a series of overlapping flat stages. The strongest tones will be in the foreground, medium tones will be in the middle ground, and the distance will become progressively paler. The English landscape artist John Sell Cotman often used this type of composition.

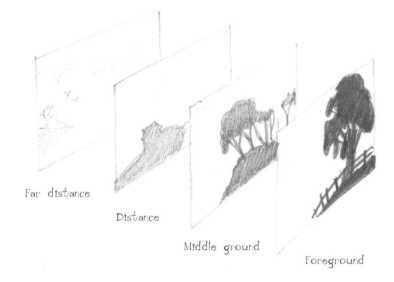

Far distance

Distance

Middle ground

Foreground

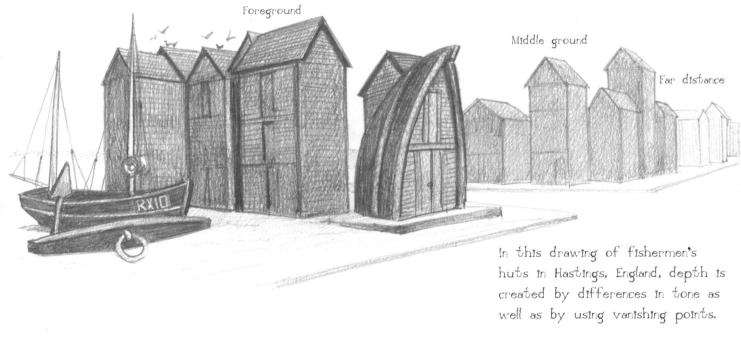

Foreground

Middle ground

Far distance

In this drawing of fishermen's huts in Hastings, England, depth is created by differences in tone as well as by using vanishing points.

31

Glossary

Centre of vision The part of the horizon that is exactly opposite the observer's viewpoint.

Cone of vision see **field of view.**

Construction lines Guidelines which are used in the earlier stages of a drawing and may be erased later.

Eye level The height of the viewer's eye above the ground plane when looking at a scene.

Field of view Everything that you can see clearly while looking straight ahead. The space between your field of view and your eye is your **cone of vision.**

Foreshortening Drawing part of an object shorter than it really is, to make it look as though it is projecting towards or away from the viewer.

Ground plane The part of a drawing that represents the ground on which the viewer stands.

Horizon The place where ground and sky appear to meet; the furthest point the eye can see. It is always at the viewer's eye level. The line in a picture that represents the horizon is the **horizon line.**

Light source The direction from which the light seems to come in a drawing.

Picture plane The surface on which the picture is drawn. Think of it as a sheet of glass, placed within the cone of vision, on which the scene is traced.

Plan view A picture of an object as it would appear if you were looking down at it from directly above, as on a map.

Vanishing point (V.P.) The place in a perspective drawing where parallel lines appear to meet.

Viewpoint The position of the viewer's eye when looking at a scene.

Index